OUR JOURNAL
From Me to You

OUR JOURNAL
From Me to You

Copyright © 2020 Mind Yours

All rights reserved.

No part of this publication may be reproduced, stored in a retrieval system, or transmitted, in any form or in any means – by electronic, mechanical, photocopying, recording or otherwise without prior written permission.

OUR JOURNAL
From Me to You

Our Journal is intended to encourage communication between parents and children through journaling, sharing thoughts, well wishes and affirmations. *Our Journal* is an instrument used for self-care that emphasizes mindfulness through activities. *Our Journal* encourages spending quality time with your child.

With this journal, a central goal is to create a safe space through open communication. There are a number of benefits in sharing this journal with your child. *Our Journal* contains activities that assist with developing emotional intelligence. It employs an emotions chart to help with identifying and articulating emotions, while using activities to teach interpersonal relationship skills. Additionally, it emphasizes problem-solving and critical thinking skills through reading and writing. It helps participants with mindfulness through drawing and coloring activities.

HERE ARE A FEW *Journaling* TIPS:

- *Our Journal* is intended to enhance communication and should be used as a tool to foster healthy relationships.

- Try to write your thoughts as clearly as possible and be open to conversations regarding journal entries.

- Ask questions if there is something that is not clear.

- It is important to leave the journal in a location where participants know where to find it (under pillow, in a drawer, on bed, etc.).

- Be consistent while using this journal. The more it is used the better the outcome.

- Use humor at times, it is not intended to always be serious. Have fun!

TOPICS INCLUDED IN
Our Journal

- Writing Prompts (to assist with topics which highlight self-care).

- Blank pages to write and draw freely.

- Coloring pages to practice mindfulness (coloring reduces stress and anxiety, improves motor skills, sleep and focus).

- List of affirmations (challenge negative thought patterns, encourage positivity and boost self-confidence).

- An emotion chart (for creating and fostering awareness of emotions helps individuals talk about and identify feelings, which ultimately helps to establish healthy relationships).

THIS JOURNAL BELONG TO:

....
....
....
....

Activity

Trace both hands on the page. Start by tracing the biggest hand first, and then trace the smaller hand inside the bigger hand. When you are finished tracing each hand, label each hand with the ages of participants at the bottom of each hand. Write about things that you have in common and things that make you different.

THINGS THAT YOU HAVE IN COMMON:

....
....
....
....
....
....

THINGS THAT MAKE YOU DIFFERENT:

....
....
....
....
....
....

Activity

Parents and children should have a way to communicate quickly when there is an emergent or urgent situation. Parents and children should create a code word so it can be used in social settings via text or verbally. When this code is used both parties should give their full attention to the person. What code word did your family choose?

WRITING PROMPTS

These writing prompts will help you to focus on a specific topic to clearly communicate your ideas. Please encourage children to draw to express themselves as that may help them communicate complex ideas and feelings.

- Draw a picture of yourself.
- Write what you like about yourself.
- What do you like most about your friends?
- What is your best family memory?
- Who do you like spending time with and why?
- I miss you during the day because….
- What is your favorite subject in school?
- If you could change anything in the world what would you change?
- What qualities do you think makes a good friend?
- When were the last time you laughed so hard that your stomach ached?
- What qualities make a best friend? What qualities make you a good friend?
- What was the best part of your day?
- What is your favorite book or movie?
- What do you do to relax?
- What was the last compliment you gave?
- What was your favorite thing about today?

GRATITUDE PROMPTS

Gratitude is focusing on and being intentional about being grateful. It has the ability to improve ones overall health. Gratitude journaling is a great way to improve, foster and develop self-respect and respect for others. Try the gratitude prompts listed below and create a daily gratitude list.

DAILY GRATITUDE THOUGHTS

- Today I will find reasons to smile.
- Today I will do something nice for a stranger.
- Today I will listen to music that brings me joy.
- Today I will look for positivity.
- Today I am happy about my freedom to…
- Today I will show gratitude to my love ones.
- Today I will think of compliments given to me and compliment others.
- Today I am grateful for a warm bed to fall asleep in every night.
- Today I will think of great memories that I share with love ones.
- Today I will be grateful for my health.
- Today I will be grateful for who I am.
- Today I am thankful that I have people who love me.

AFFIRMATIONS

Affirmations are short powerful statements that shape our reality. Affirmations help you think about and speak into existence the things you want to achieve. Affirmations also help you to acknowledge the amazing things that are already present in your life. The purpose of affirmations are to encourage positive thinking and speaking about our own lives and the lives of those we love. It is important to write, speak and think about our desires so our minds can visualize a plan. Here are simple empowering affirmations that will have impactful affects on the conscious and unconscious mind.

Child

I can make a difference

I like myself

I can do it

I am brave

My smile brightens everything around me

I love to try new things

I can reach my goals

My feelings are important because they matter

I believe in myself

My life matters

I accept myself exactly as I am

Parent to Child

I love you

I am proud of you

I am praying for you

You are safe with me

You are brave

I love hanging out with you

You inspire me

You are a joy to be around

You brighten up my day

You are so smart

You are amazing

Parent

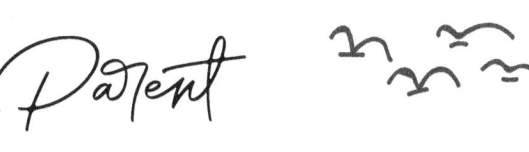

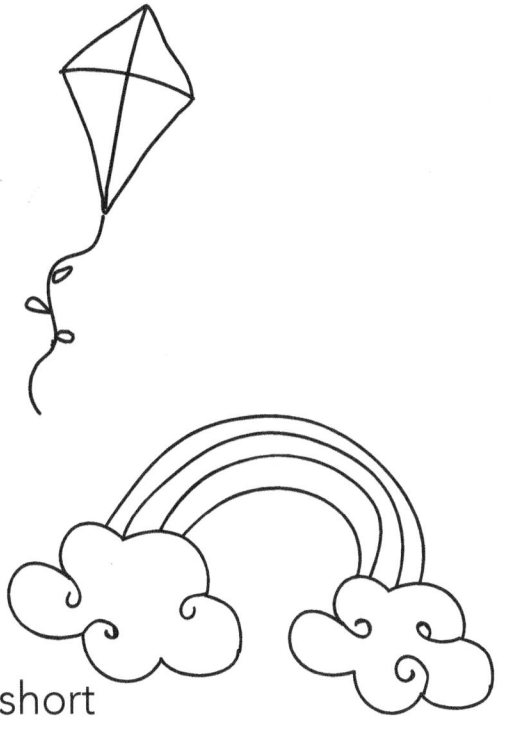

I am a good parent

It is ok to ask for help

The days are long but the years are short

I am present & in the moment with you

I show love through my actions and words

I am learning along the way

I am not just a parent

I laugh with my children

Taking care of myself is not selfish

I am exactly who and what my child needs

Emotion & FEELING CHART

This chart is beneficial for children and their caregivers to examine how occasions and moods can affect emotions. Emotion charts help increase emotional vocabulary and assist children to make connections about their feelings.

USE THIS CHART FOR THE FOLLOWING ACTIVITIES:

1. Understanding Empathy:

A. Discuss current events, TV shows or movies. What was noticed about the character's behavior? Choose an emotion from the chart that you noticed a character portrayed? What are better ways to handle the situation?

Example: The book, *The Three Little Pigs*. How do you think the pigs felt when the wolf continued to blow their house down? How do you think the wolf felt about chasing the pigs? How did the pigs feel?

2. Identify Coping Skills:

A. Discuss coping skills by choosing an emotion from the chart and then ask, what physiological feelings (heart rate, warm sensation, sweat, butterflies, etc.) are present in the body when experiencing the chosen feeling or emotion?

B. Pick an emotion that you experienced today by writing, drawing and talking about the way you dealt with it.

C. List things you like to do when you are happy, angry or sad.

3. Choose an emotion on the chart, after that list emotions that have similar meaning to the one you chose. Then list emotions that are opposite. Notice how many new emotions you are able to come up with.

Example: Happy is listed on the emotion chart but ecstatic is not. Ecstatic is an emotion that also means happy.

Emotion/ FEELING CHART

ADMIRATION	AMUSEMENT	ANGER	ANXIOUS

AWKWARD	BORED	CALM	CONTENT

DISGUST	EXCITEMENT	FEAR	HAPPY

JEALOUS	JOY	LAZY	MAD

ROMANCE	SAD	SCARED	SURPRISE

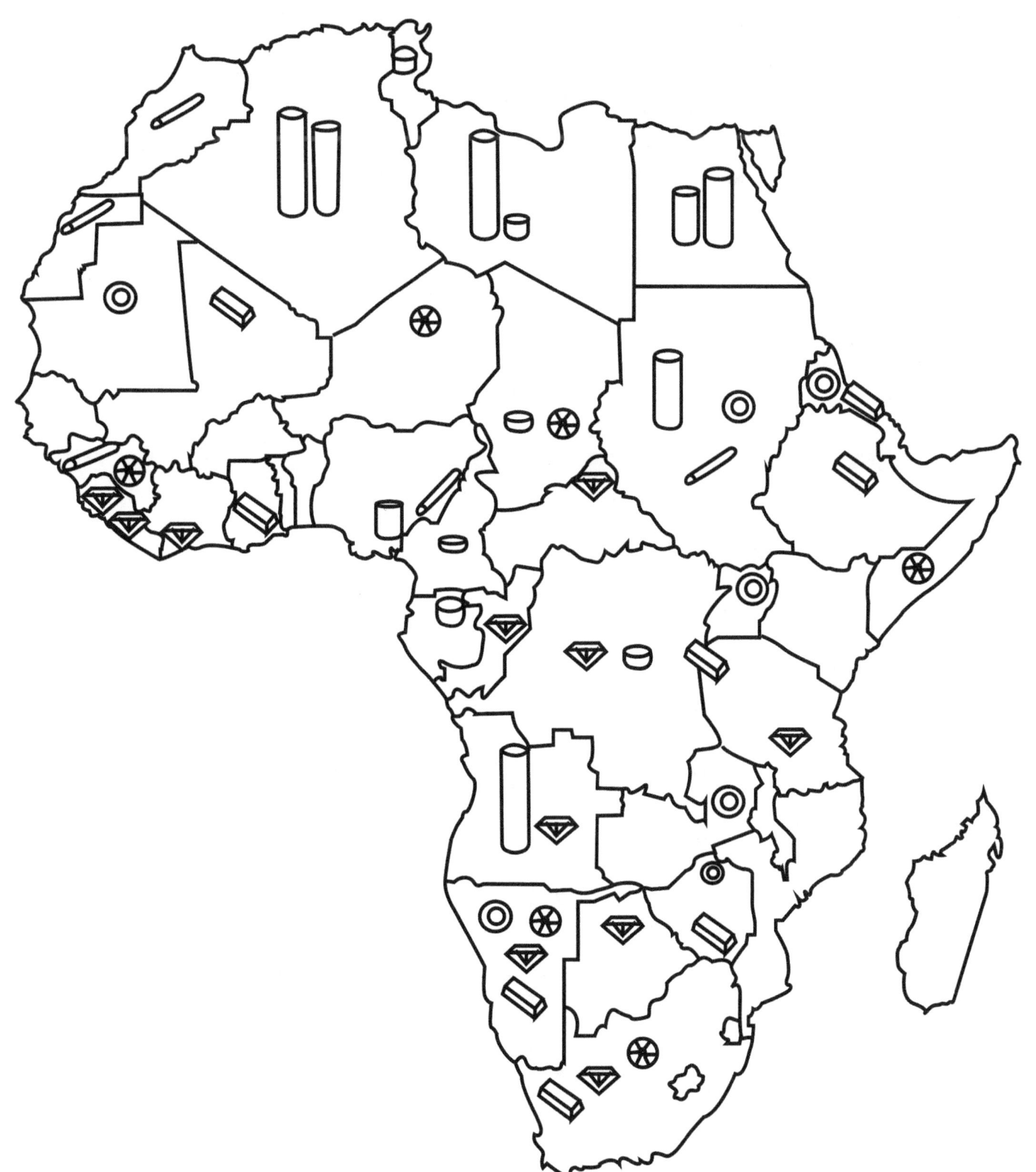

ABOUT THE AUTHOR

Katie Onitiri-Hageman is a mother of two astonishing boys and wants the absolute best for them. She is a wife; therapist, entrepreneur and a community advocate who often feels guilt for not staying at home full-time to care for her children. She has come to understand that many parents experience similar guilt. An important goal for Katie is to normalize discussing the guilt that parents feel and encourage them to spend meaningful memorable time with their families. She believes that parents deserve a balanced life, even when having to balance many demands. Katie developed ideas that enhanced quality time. She implements time with her boys that are intimate, memorable, educational and fun. She created this journal to share those ideas and positive experiences with other parents. Katie advocates self-care and encourages parents to apply self-care in their lives to be better caregivers.

Please visit **www.adeselfcare.com**
for additional resources.

www.ingramcontent.com/pod-product-compliance
Lightning Source LLC
Chambersburg PA
CBHW081155290426
44108CB00018B/2559